TOP TRUMPS
ULTIMATE
CARS 2

This book is officially licensed by Winning Moves UK Ltd, owners of the Top Trumps registered trademark.

Richard Dredge has asserted his right to be identified as the author of this book.

First published in August 2008

British Library Cataloguing-in-Publication Data:
A catalogue record for this book is available from the British Library

ISBN 978 1 84425 641 9

Library of Congress catalog card no. 2008929393

Published by Haynes Publishing,
Sparkford, Yeovil, Somerset BA22 7JJ, UK
Tel: 01963 442030 Fax: 01963 440001
Int. tel: +44 1963 442030 Int. fax: +44 1963 440001
Email: sales@haynes.co.uk
Website: www.haynes.co.uk

Haynes North America, Inc.,
861 Lawrence Drive, Newbury Park, California 91320, USA

Printed and bound in Great Britain by J. H. Haynes & Co. Ltd, Sparkford

Photographic credits:
All photographs sourced from www.magiccarpics.co.uk

The Author

Richard Dredge got addicted to cars when he was a child, rebuilding his first Triumph at 16. He contributes to publications such as *Octane*, *Practical Classics* and *Auto Express*. For a fuller CV, look at www.richarddredge.com

TOP TRUMPS®
ULTIMATE CARS 2

Contents

About
Top Trumps

It's now more than 30 years since Britain's kids first caught the Top Trumps craze. The game remained hugely popular until the 1990s, when it slowly drifted into obscurity. Then, in 1999, UK games company Winning Moves discovered it, bought it, dusted it down, gave it a thorough makeover and introduced it to a whole new generation. And so the Top Trumps legend continues.

Nowadays, there are Top Trumps titles for just about everyone, with subjects about animals, cars, ships, aircraft and all the great films and TV shows. Top Trumps is now even more popular than before. In Britain, a pack of Top Trumps is bought every six seconds! And it's not just British children who love the game. Children in Australasia, the Far East, the Middle East, all over Europe and in North America can buy Top Trumps at their local shops.

Today you can even play the game on the internet, interactive DVD, your games console and even your mobile phone.

You've played the game...

Now read the book!

Haynes Publishing and Top Trumps have teamed up to bring you this exciting new Top Trumps book, in which you will find even more pictures, details and statistics.

Top Trumps: Ultimate Cars 2 features 45 of the world's most exciting road cars, ranging from the stunning Alfa Romeo 8C to the timeless Porsche 911 GT2 and the brutal Dodge Viper RT/10. Packed with fascinating facts, stunning photographs and all the vital statistics, this is the essential pocket guide.

Look out for other Top Trumps books from Haynes Publishing – even more facts, even more fun!

Alfa Romeo
8C
Alfa returns to greatness

Alfa Romeo
8C

Alfa returns to greatness

Take a Maserati V8 engine, wrap it up in one of the most seductive shapes ever created and you have Alfa Romeo's 8C. But it nearly didn't happen; the company was too busy trying to sort out how to split Maserati and Ferrari while also entering the American market. Thankfully the company persisted with the project, which has the go to match the show – this isn't a car that's all mouth and no trousers. It's a good job the 8C happened; just 500 cars are being made, with each one sold before the first example had even been built. Alfa has now got such a taste for success that it has unveiled an open-topped edition, which will no doubt sell out even faster.

Statistics

Price	£120,000
0–60mph	4.2sec
0–100mph	8.0sec (est)
Max speed	190mph (304kph)
Engine type	V8
Engine capacity	4691cc
Bore x stroke	94mm x 84.5mm
Max power	450bhp @ 7000rpm
Max torque	354lb ft @ 4750rpm
Power to weight ratio	284bhp per tonne
Transmission	Six-speed manual, rear-wheel drive
Kerb weight	1585kg
Length	4278mm
Width	1900mm
Height	1250mm
Fuel consumption	18mpg
Year introduced	2008

AR 008 EU

Alpina (BMW Z8)
Roadster

From bruiser to cruiser

Alpina (BMW Z8)
Roadster

From bruiser to cruiser

Packing a 5-litre M5 V8 up front, you could hardly accuse the standard BMW Z8 of being limp-wristed. That didn't stop Alpina from producing 555 examples of its own edition though, with even more striking looks thanks to 20-inch alloy wheels and a choice of bright metallic finishes. However, while the car packed more show, there wasn't as much go as the standard offering, as Alpina did something unusual: it made the Z8 more of a cruiser and less of a hard-core driver's car. To that end it installed a slightly smaller (4.8-litre) V8 with less power but more torque, which was also mated to an automatic gearbox.

Statistics

Price	£86,000
0–62mph	5.3sec
0–100mph	9.5sec (est)
Max speed	155mph (248kph)
Engine type	V8
Engine capacity	4837cc
Bore x stroke	93mm x 89mm
Max power	381bhp @ 5800rpm
Max torque	383lb ft @ 3800rpm
Power to weight ratio	235bhp per tonne
Transmission	Five-speed auto, rear-wheel drive
Kerb weight	1620kg
Length	4400mm
Width	1830mm
Height	1317mm
Fuel consumption	21.4mpg
Year introduced	2003

OAL V8

Ascari
KZ-1

Britain's greatest supercar secret

Ascari
KZ-1

Britain's greatest supercar secret

Although it was first shown as long ago as 2000, the KZ-1 seems to be undergoing constant development to the point where it's not clear whether or not there will ever be a definitive finished car. However, the basic specification of the Ascari has always been a mid-mounted 5-litre BMW V8 engine, taken from the M5 – which is never going to be a bad starting point. Thanks to a carbon-fibre bodyshell, the car is lighter than most rivals (and even some superminis), ensuring agility and phenomenal pace. Buy one and you could even use it for track days on Ascari's own circuit in Spain.

Statistics

Price	**£235,000**
0–60mph	**3.8sec**
0–100mph	**8.3sec**
Max speed	**200mph (320kph) (est)**
Engine type	**V8**
Engine capacity	**4941cc**
Bore x stroke	**94mm x 89mm**
Max power	**500bhp @ 7000rpm**
Max torque	**368lb ft @ 4500rpm**
Power to weight ratio	**392bhp per tonne**
Transmission	**Six-speed manual, rear-wheel drive**
Kerb weight	**1275kg**
Length	**4300mm**
Width	**1852mm**
Height	**1138mm**
Fuel consumption	**18mpg**
Year introduced	**2000**

Aston Martin
DBS

Aston's transformation is complete

Aston Martin
DBS

Aston's transformation is complete

As soon as Aston Martin introduced the DB7 in 1993, it was clear that the company was once again destined for great things. The DB9 was even better and while the Vanquish had proved to be a missed opportunity, its replacement, the DBS largely made up for any lost ground. Lithe and beautiful, the DBS is packed with subtle touches that enable the most to be made of the 6-litre V12 up front. It's also the first Aston Martin to make extensive use of carbon-fibre in its construction; the DBS benefits from experience gained in the design and building of the DBR9 and DBRS9 racing cars.

Price	£160,000
0–62mph	4.2sec
0–100mph	8.7sec
Max speed	194mph (310kph)
Engine type	V12
Engine capacity	5935cc
Bore x stroke	89.0mm x 79.5mm
Max power	510bhp @ 6500rpm
Max torque	420lb ft @ 5750rpm
Power to weight ratio	301bhp per tonne
Transmission	Six-speed manual, rear-wheel drive
Kerb weight	1695kg
Length	4721mm
Width	1905mm
Height	1280mm
Fuel consumption	17.3mpg
Year introduced	2008

Audi
Quattro Sport
Greased lightning

Audi
Quattro Sport

Greased lightning

You could be forgiven for thinking that the Sport was merely a
shortened Quattro, but it was far more than that. Up front was an
all-alloy engine in place of the usual cast-iron unit, to save weight;
with the same aim, the standard steel bodywork was junked in
favour of carbon fibre and kevlar panels. The short wheelbase
ensured greater agility, while the turbocharger was tweaked to give
massive boost – and even more massive amounts of lag. The result
though was upwards of 450bhp for the racing editions, and thanks
to ultra-short gearing, the available acceleration could put the
Porsche 911 Turbo in the shade.

Statistics

Price	£55,000
0–60mph	4.8sec
0–100mph	12.6sec
Max speed	155mph (248kph)
Engine type	In-line five
Engine capacity	2134cc
Bore x stroke	79.3mm x 86.4mm
Max power	306bhp @ 6700rpm
Max torque	258lb ft @ 3700rpm
Power to weight ratio	240bhp per tonne
Transmission	Five-speed manual, four-wheel drive
Kerb weight	1273kg
Length	4160mm
Width	1780mm
Height	1345mm
Fuel consumption	15.3mpg
Year introduced	1984

Bentley
Brooklands

Crewe's missile

Bentley
Brooklands

Crewe's missile

If you subscribe to the theory that biggest is best, the Brooklands is the best car ever made. Everything about it is massive: its engine, wheels and brakes, interior – the list goes on. While Bentley's sales figures have been boosted by the almost mass-produced Continental GT, the Brooklands harks back to the company's glory days, with everything fettled by hand – so the £250,000 price tag makes this car appear a relative bargain. However, one thing that's not quite so big is the production run; with just 550 examples offered during a three-year production run, the Brooklands will never be a common sight on the road.

Statistics

Price	£230,000
0–60mph	5.0sec
0–100mph	11.6sec
Max speed	184mph (294kph)
Engine type	V8
Engine capacity	6761cc
Bore x stroke	104.2mm x 99.1mm
Max power	530bhp @ 4000rpm
Max torque	774lb ft @ 3200rpm
Power to weight ratio	199bhp per tonne
Transmission	Six-speed auto, rear-wheel drive
Kerb weight	2665kg
Length	5411mm
Width	2078mm
Height	1473mm
Fuel consumption	14.5mpg
Year introduced	2008

Bentley
Continental GT Speed

From cruiser to bruiser

Bentley
Continental GT Speed

From cruiser to bruiser

Easily Bentley's best-selling car ever, the Continental GT has taken the company places it has never been before. However, while the standard GT is classy and swift, it's no driver's car; the Speed is intended to change that. Offering more power and torque, plus a lower kerb weight than the standard edition, the Speed offers more agility – not least because the suspension has been retuned to reduce roll without compromising the ride. It's not just about go though; a bit of extra show never goes amiss. To that end the Speed features a slightly more aggressive nose than usual plus a raft of interior upgrades such as drilled pedals and quilted leather trim.

Statistics

Price	**£137,500**
0–60mph	**4.3sec**
0–100mph	**10.5sec (est)**
Max speed	**203mph (325kph)**
Engine type	**W12**
Engine capacity	**5998cc**
Bore x stroke	**84mm x 90.2mm**
Max power	**602bhp @ 6000rpm**
Max torque	**553lb ft @ 1750rpm**
Power to weight ratio	**256bhp per tonne**
Transmission	**Six-speed auto, four-wheel drive**
Kerb weight	**2350kg**
Length	**4804mm**
Width	**1916mm**
Height	**1380mm**
Fuel consumption	**17.0mpg**
Year introduced	**2007**

BMW
M1

The supercar that came too late

BMW M1

The supercar that came too late

Compare the M1's specification with other cars in these pages and you won't be impressed, but when launched, this was a mid-engined monster to give Ferrari and Lamborghini the shakes. The M1 was originally designed as a track car, but to qualify for entry in Group 4 racing, 400 road examples would also have to be constructed. The design was based on a dramatic 1972 BMW gull-winged concept called the Turbo, but with the styling toned down a bit. The car still looked amazing though, so it was a shame that the project ran so late that by the time it appeared, the Group 4 series had been scrapped.

Statistics

Price	£37,640
0–62mph	5.5sec
0–100mph	13.0sec
Max speed	162mph (259kph)
Engine type	In-line six
Engine capacity	3453cc
Bore x stroke	93.4mm x 84.0mm
Max power	277bhp @ 6500rpm
Max torque	239lb ft @ 5000rpm
Power to weight ratio	195bhp per tonne
Transmission	Five-speed manual, rear-wheel drive
Kerb weight	1418kg
Length	4360mm
Width	1820mm
Height	1140mm
Fuel consumption	17.0mpg
Year introduced	1980

BMW
M6

Not pretty, but seriously quick

BMW M6

Not pretty, but seriously quick

M · DY 4262

Continuing BMW's trend for naming its cars after British motorways, the M6 took the M5's fabulous V10 engine and mated it with the not-very-pretty 6-Series bodyshell to come up with a truly special driver's car. Much more costly than the more practical M5 saloon and Touring, the M6 is lighter, lower and wider, with a slightly shorter wheelbase for added agility. The weight has been saved by adopting a carbon-fibre roof plus forged aluminium wheels along with thinner glass for the rear screen; this is a car that's designed to eat continents whole, while providing masses of fun along the way.

Statistics

Price	£80,755
0–60mph	4.7sec
0–100mph	9.7sec
Max speed	155mph (248kph)
Engine type	V10
Engine capacity	4999cc
Bore x stroke	92.0mm x 75.2mm
Max power	500bhp @ 7750rpm
Max torque	384lb ft @ 6100rpm
Power to weight ratio	296bhp per tonne
Transmission	Seven-speed manual, rear-wheel drive
Kerb weight	1785kg
Length	4871mm
Width	2043mm
Height	1372mm
Fuel consumption	14.8mpg
Year introduced	2005

M·DY 4262

Bristol
Fighter T

Quirky British company goes its own way

Bristol
Fighter T

Quirky British company goes its own way

Bristol has never felt that it needs to go with the flow; it's one of those companies that does things its own way, for a very select number of appreciative buyers. Nowhere is that more evident than with the Fighter, with its gull-wing doors, narrow bodyshell and Chrysler Viper V10 engine in the nose. Even the standard car can top 210mph thanks to its 525bhp, but for those who feel that too much power is not enough, the Fighter T was unveiled in 2007. With a claimed 1012bhp, the car can theoretically manage 270mph – but it's electronically limited to a 'more than sufficient' 225mph.

Statistics

Price	£351,931
0–62mph	3.5sec
0–100mph	7.5sec (est)
Max speed	225mph (360kph)
Engine type	V10
Engine capacity	7996cc
Bore x stroke	101.6mm x 98.6mm
Max power	1012bhp @ 5600rpm
Max torque	1036lb ft @ 4500rpm
Power to weight ratio	340bhp per tonne
Transmission	Six-speed manual, rear-wheel drive
Kerb weight	1540kg
Length	4420mm
Width	1795mm
Height	1345mm
Fuel consumption	14mpg
Year introduced	2007

Bugatti
EB110

The supercar that nearly never was

Bugatti
EB110

The supercar that nearly never was

Bugatti's revival is now complete, with the Veyron grabbing headlines everywhere and no standard production car likely to take its crown. However, around 15 years before the Veyron appeared, Bugatti tried a similar trick but failed spectacularly when its EB110 arrived. It took two years just to secure the rights to use the Bugatti name, then a factory was built in Italy's supercar country, Modena, with an impressive team of great engineers and designers drafted in to see the project through. Aerospace technology was used thanks to a tie-up with French company Aerospatiale, but despite power, performance and looks aplenty, Bugatti couldn't make the car economically.

Statistics

Price	**£285,500**
0–62mph	**3.4sec**
0–100mph	**9.6sec**
Max speed	**214mph (342kph)**
Engine type	**V12**
Engine capacity	**3500cc**
Bore x stroke	**81mm x 57mm**
Max power	**560bhp @ 8000rpm**
Max torque	**451lb ft @ 3750rpm**
Power to weight ratio	**345bhp per tonne**
Transmission	**Six-speed manual, four-wheel drive**
Kerb weight	**1566kg**
Length	**4400mm**
Width	**1940mm**
Height	**1125mm**
Fuel consumption	**18.8mpg**
Year introduced	**1992**

Cadillac
Sixteen

It's got the torque of the devil

Cadillac
Sixteen

It's got the torque of the devil

With massively powerful and luxurious concepts being unveiled
at every motor show, Cadillac needed to pull out all the stops
to produce something that stood out at the 2003 Detroit event.
The result was a car that upstaged every other exhibit – and
quite rightly so when you consider the car's specification.
With a huge V16 engine up front, there was 1000bhp
on tap – although as a token gesture towards the
environmentalists there was 'displacement on
demand'. This allowed up to 12 of the cylinders to
be shut down in a bid to conserve fuel; a feature
that's fitted to many of GM's production cars.

Statistics

Price	N/A
0–62mph	3.8sec (est)
0–100mph	6.5sec (est)
Max speed	190mph (304kph) (est)
Engine type	V16
Engine capacity	13,600cc
Bore x stroke	105mm x 98mm
Max power	1000bhp @ 6000rpm
Max torque	1000lb ft @ 4300rpm
Power to weight ratio	440bhp per tonne
Transmission	Four-speed automatic, rear-wheel drive
Kerb weight	2270kg
Length	5673mm
Width	2058mm
Height	1392mm
Fuel consumption	15mpg (est)
Year introduced	2003

Chrysler
ME4I2

Serious tech from the US of A

Chrysler
ME412

Serious tech from the US of A

When Chrylser unveiled its ME412 at the 2004 Detroit Motor Show, the company went to great pains to point out that the car could enter production within six months. There was an 850bhp quad-turbo Mercedes-sourced V12 in the middle, with just the rear wheels being driven via a twin-clutch seven-speed gearbox. However, Chrysler knew that making the car reliable and usable would consume huge amounts of cash – and it was money that the company didn't have. So it was no surprise when Chrysler pulled the plug, just before things started to go badly wrong for the company, ultimately leading to its split from Mercedes.

Statistics

Price	N/A
0–62mph	2.9sec
0–100mph	6.2sec
Max speed	248mph (397kph)
Engine type	V12
Engine capacity	5980cc
Bore x stroke	82.6mm x 93mm
Max power	850bhp @ 5750rpm
Max torque	850lb ft @ 2500rpm
Power to weight ratio	649bhp per tonne
Transmission	Seven-speed manual, rear-wheel drive
Kerb weight	1310kg
Length	4542mm
Width	1999mm
Height	1140mm
Fuel consumption	14mpg (est)
Year introduced	2004

Lizeta
VI6T

Meet the ultimate, ultimate car

TO · 67661M

Cizeta
V16T

Meet the ultimate, ultimate car

If supercars are about extremes, this must be the ultimate, thanks to a crazy 5995cc 16-cylinder engine – transversely mounted! No wonder the Cizeta was so wide; it had eight cylinders across its girth. With 560bhp at a dizzying 8000rpm, the noise was awe-inspiring at full chat, thanks to 64 valves doing their stuff. It was claimed the V16T could top 204mph, but nobody ever officially tested the car, so who knows? Despite the prototype emerging in 1989, it was 1992 before the first cars were ready; in the meantime, financier Giorgio Moroder walked away, but the car lingered on until 1995.

Statistics

Price	£333,900
0–62mph	4.4sec
0–100mph	12.0sec
Max speed	204mph (326kph)
Engine type	V16
Engine capacity	5995cc
Bore x stroke	86mm x 65mm
Max power	560bhp @ 8000rpm
Max torque	469lb ft @ 6000rpm
Power to weight ratio	329bhp per tonne
Transmission	Five-speed manual, rear-wheel drive
Kerb weight	1600kg
Length	4440mm
Width	2050mm
Height	1120mm
Fuel consumption	18mpg
Year introduced	1991

De Tomaso
Pantera
Italian design with American V8 power

De Tomaso
Pantera
Italian design with American V8 power

As the 1970s dawned, Ford realised that it needed something
to boost its image. After the success of the GT40, a mid-
engined supercar was just the ticket, but instead of
developing one in-house, Italian car maker De Tomaso was
commissioned to do the work. In 1970 a prototype was shown,
with the car entering production in 1971. Naturally there was
a Ford V8 installed, which drove the rear wheels via a five-
speed gearbox – two V6 protypes were also made but they
never entered production. In reality the Pantera was usually
appallingly badly built – but when you've got looks like those,
who cares about shut lines or blistering paint?

Statistics

Price	**£47,621**
0–62mph	**5.4sec**
0–100mph	**13.1sec**
Max speed	**165mph (264kph)**
Engine type	**V8**
Engine capacity	**5763cc**
Bore x stroke	**101.6mm x 88.9mm**
Max power	**350bhp @ 6000rpm**
Max torque	**333lb ft @ 3800rpm**
Power to weight ratio	**240bhp per tonne**
Transmission	**Five-speed manual, rear-wheel drive**
Kerb weight	**1460kg**
Length	**4269mm**
Width	**1968mm**
Height	**1099mm**
Fuel consumption	**16mpg**
Year introduced	**1971**

Dodge
Viper RT/10

Proof that too much is not enough

KL54 CWX

Dodge
Viper RT/IO

Proof that too much is not enough

There's an old adage which claims there's no substitute for cubic inches, and here's the proof. You'll have to search long and hard to find a production road car that's got an engine bigger than the Dodge's 8.4-litre V10; this is a machine where brute force rules, rather than cutting-edge sophistication. The original production Viper surfaced in 1992, but by 2004 there was a rebodied edition. However, there may have been a new set of clothes, but massive performance was still the number one priority – and for 2008 there's even more urge, thanks to a monster 8.4-litre engine with even more power and torque than before.

Statistics

Price	$87,500
0–62mph	3.5sec
0–100mph	7.6sec
Max speed	197mph (315kph)
Engine type	V10
Engine capacity	8354cc
Bore x stroke	103mm x 100.6mm
Max power	600bhp @ 6100rpm
Max torque	560lb ft @ 5000rpm
Power to weight ratio	385bhp per tonne
Transmission	Six-speed manual, rear-wheel drive
Kerb weight	1560kg
Length	4459mm
Width	1911mm
Height	1210mm
Fuel consumption	14mpg
Year introduced	2003

Ferrari
599GTB

Maranello's best ever road car?

GB

Ferrari
599GTB

Maranello's best ever road car?

Not all Ferrari's V12 monsters have been truly great, but the 599GTB ranks easily as the best 12-cylinder car it's ever built. With its long bonnet and perfect proportions, this is a genuinely worthy successor to the 575M. Crucially though, the 599GTB isn't just about looks; cutting-edge engineering ensures stunning performance too. An all-aluminium chassis reduces weight and maintains rigidity, while the stiffness of the dampers can be adjusted by steering wheel-mounted buttons. Throw in carbon-ceramic brakes and an F1-style paddle-shift gearchange and it makes previous Ferrari V12s, such as the Testarossa, look like they came from another century. Oh wait, they did...

Statistics

Price	£184,980
0–62mph	3.7sec
0–100mph	7.4sec
Max speed	205mph (328kph)
Engine type	V12
Engine capacity	5999cc
Bore x stroke	92mm x 75.2mm
Max power	611bhp @ 7600rpm
Max torque	448lb ft @ 5600rpm
Power to weight ratio	362bhp per tonne
Transmission	Six-speed semi-auto, rear-wheel drive
Kerb weight	1690kg
Length	4665mm
Width	1962mm
Height	1336mm
Fuel consumption	11.8mpg
Year introduced	2006

Ford
GT40

Ford's finest hour

GNB 787D

Ford
GT40
Ford's finest hour

GNB 787D

Ford was all set to buy Ferrari in 1963, then the rug was pulled from underneath them at the last minute. In a fit of pique the company decided it would thrash Ferrari where it mattered most: on the race track. The GT40 was the result, and to say it succeeded in belittling Ferrari is one of the all-time great understatements. The start point was a Lola V8-powered prototype which had retired from the 1963 24 Hours. However, a complete rethink by Ford's Advanced Vehicle Operations ensured victory would be Ford's, with the GT40 winning Le Mans in 1966, 1968 and 1969, the last two in private hands.

Statistics

Price	**£6,647**
0–60mph	**5.3sec**
0–100mph	**10sec (est)**
Max speed	**164mph (262kph)**
Engine type	**V8**
Engine capacity	**4736cc**
Bore x stroke	**101.7mm x 72.9mm**
Max power	**335bhp @ 6250rpm**
Max torque	**329lb ft @ 3200rpm**
Power to weight ratio	**360bhp per tonne**
Transmission	**Five-speed manual, rear-wheel drive**
Kerb weight	**931kg**
Length	**4181mm**
Width	**1778mm**
Height	**1029mm**
Fuel consumption	**12mpg**
Year introduced	**1964**

Ford
RS200

Group B hero

Ford
RS200

Group B hero

In the 1980s, when it came to insane levels of performance – at least in terms of acceleration and agility – nothing could match a Group B rally car. Some of the most powerful racing machines ever devised, Group B cars packed the most cutting-edge technology in terms of materials and construction. Nowhere was this more evident than with Ford's RS200, with its aluminium honeycomb and composite bodyshell. The best bit though was that for the cars to qualify in Group B, a series of road cars also had to be built, and while the RS200 wasn't easy to live with, it could eat Porsches for breakfast!

Statistics

Price	£49,995
0–62mph	6.1sec
0–100mph	17sec
Max speed	140mph (224kph)
Engine type	In-line four
Engine capacity	1803cc
Bore x stroke	86mm x 77.6mm
Max power	250bhp @ 6000rpm
Max torque	215lb ft @ 4000rpm
Power to weight ratio	211bhp per tonne
Transmission	Five-speed manual, rear-wheel drive
Kerb weight	1180kg
Length	4000mm
Width	1752mm
Height	Variable
Fuel consumption	18mpg
Year introduced	1984

Invicta
S1

A missed opportunity

WM03 BXN

Invicta
S1

A missed opportunity

It doesn't matter that the S1 seems to have quietly died, with nobody noticing; what matters is that it ever existed at all. This car summed up everything that's great about tiny British car makers, all those blokes in sheds knocking out yet another hypercar with implausible claims about performance and production numbers. The Invicta was especially fascinating in this regard; it offered anything from relatively mild (320bhp) to truly wild (600bhp) options, with hopes of 20 cars being sold each year. But with such capable machinery elsewhere from blue-chip supercar builders, Invicta never stood a chance, and nobody even noticed the company arrive in 2003, then quietly disappear.

Statistics

Price	£150,000
0–62mph	3.8sec
0–100mph	9.1sec
Max speed	200mph (320kph)
Engine type	V8
Engine capacity	4600cc
Bore x stroke	90.2mm x 90mm
Max power	600bhp @ 4500rpm
Max torque	575lb ft @ 4500rpm
Power to weight ratio	435bhp per tonne
Transmission	Five-speed manual, rear-wheel drive
Kerb weight	1380kg
Length	4400mm
Width	2000mm
Height	1225mm
Fuel consumption	22mpg
Year introduced	2003

Lamborghini
Gallardo LP560

Beauty with brains

Lamborghini
Gallardo LP560

Beauty with brains

Until now, supercars haven't ever been about being green; they've always been about throwing as much petrol into a multi-cylinder engine as possible, in a bid to produce the greatest amount of power. Not the Gallardo LP560-4 though, which may look like previous editions of Lamborghini's baby supercar – but in reality it's an object lesson in efficiency. Not only is the car much more aerodynamic, but the engine and transmission are far more efficient too. Meanwhile the suspension has also been given a thorough reworking to ensure the most can be made of the extra power offered by the enlarged engine. Proof that you can have beauty as well as brains.

Statistics

Price	£147,330
0–62mph	3.7sec
0–100mph	8.0sec (est)
Max speed	203mph (325kph)
Engine type	V10
Engine capacity	5204cc
Bore x stroke	84.5mm x 92.8mm
Max power	560bhp @ 8000rpm
Max torque	398lb ft @ 6500rpm
Power to weight ratio	398bhp per tonne
Transmission	Six-speed manual, four-wheel drive
Kerb weight	1410kg
Length	4345mm
Width	1900mm
Height	1165mm
Fuel consumption	19.2mpg
Year introduced	2008

Lotec
Sirius

Seriously exclusive supercar

Lotec
Sirius

Seriously exclusive supercar

Kurt Lotterschmid's first creation, the C1000 of 1992, didn't leave much of an impression on the supercar world. Unfortunately it seems his follow up, the 2004 Sirius, is likely to suffer a similar fate, as his company can produce no more than five cars each year. Still, it's making each one count as even in basic form there's 850bhp on tap and the promise of well over 200mph. Opt for the longer final drive and higher boost pressures (there are two turbos strapped to the Mercedes-sourced V12) and there's a scarcely believable 1200bhp on offer. And it's all at half the price of a Veyron...

Statistics

Price	£380,000
0–62mph	3.8sec
0–100mph	6.2sec (est)
Max speed	242mph (387kph)
Engine type	V12
Engine capacity	5987cc
Bore x stroke	98mm x 80.2mm
Max power	1200bhp @ 6300rpm
Max torque	974lb ft @ 3400rpm
Power to weight ratio	938bhp per tonne
Transmission	Six-speed manual, rear-wheel drive
Kerb weight	1280kg
Length	4120mm
Width	2080mm
Height	1120mm
Fuel consumption	12mpg
Year introduced	2004

Lotus
Elise SC

Improving on perfection

Lotus
Elise SC

Improving on perfection

When it comes to affordable and (relatively) practical performance cars, nothing can touch the Elise. One of the best-handling cars ever conceived, the baby Lotus is fast and a blast on every drive. Even the first-generation cars have sublime handling, but the second-generation edition is even better, and for those who felt the chassis could handle more power, here's the proof. With the 1.8-litre Toyota engine now supercharged to give 217bhp, the car is a better driver's tool than ever, while the styling has also been sharpened up by the addition of an integrated rear spoiler and fresh alloy wheels. It's hard to see how Lotus will improve on this one!

Statistics

Price	**£32,500**
0–62mph	**4.4sec**
0–100mph	**10.7sec**
Max speed	**150mph (240kph)**
Engine type	**In-line four**
Engine capacity	**1796cc**
Bore x stroke	**79mm x 91.5mm**
Max power	**217bhp @ 8000rpm**
Max torque	**155lb ft @ 5000rpm**
Power to weight ratio	**240bhp per tonne**
Transmission	**Six-speed manual, rear-wheel drive**
Kerb weight	**903kg**
Length	**3785mm**
Width	**1720mm**
Height	**1120mm**
Fuel consumption	**31mpg**
Year introduced	**2008**

Lotus
Carlton

Hyper saloon number one

Lotus
Carlton

Hyper saloon number one

Although insanely fast and powerful family cars are now on every street corner, in the early '90s there was just one place to go if you wanted to transport five people at warp speed: your local Vauxhall dealer. Capable of nearly 180mph thanks to some serious fettling by Lotus, this Carlton generated newspaper headlines it was so quick. The original idea had been to slot the Corvette ZR-1's V8 into the engine bay, but when it wouldn't fit, Lotus increased the Carlton GSi's engine displacement to 3.6 litres, bolted on a pair of turbochargers and hey presto; the world's fastest and most powerful saloon.

Statistics

Price	£48,000
0–62mph	5.1sec
0–100mph	11.1sec
Max speed	177mph (283kph)
Engine type	In-line six
Engine capacity	3615cc
Bore x stroke	95mm x 85mm
Max power	377bhp @ 5200rpm
Max torque	419lb ft @ 4200rpm
Power to weight ratio	228bhp per tonne
Transmission	Six-speed manual, rear-wheel drive
Kerb weight	1655kg
Length	4768mm
Width	1933mm
Height	1435mm
Fuel consumption	14.3mpg
Year introduced	1990

Maserati
MC12

For when an Enzo is too common

Maserati
MC12

For when an Enzo is too common

Although Maserati is a marque that was founded on racing, the MC12 marked a return to the race tracks for the Italian company, after more than half a century. If it hadn't been for the Ferrari Enzo, upon which the MC12 was based, the return would probably never have happened. The MC12 donated its carbon fibre and nomex honeycomb monocoque, along with its mid-mounted V12, but with the latter reworked to reduce power and torque slightly. That meant its top speed was also down on the Enzo's to just 205mph – but that didn't stop the production run of 50 from selling out instantly.

Statistics

Price	$770,000
0–62mph	3.8sec
0–100mph	6.5sec (est)
Max speed	205mph (328kph)
Engine type	V12
Engine capacity	5998cc
Bore x stroke	92mm x 75.2mm
Max power	622bhp @ 7500rpm
Max torque	480lb ft @ 5500rpm
Power to weight ratio	473bhp per tonne
Transmission	Six-speed manual, rear-wheel drive
Kerb weight	1335kg
Length	5143mm
Width	2100mm
Height	1205mm
Fuel consumption	17mpg (est)
Year introduced	2005

Mercedes
300 SL

Speed with elegance

Mercedes
300 SL

Speed with elegance

Despite those space-age looks and mechanical fuel injection, the Mercedes 300 SL wasn't really that advanced technically. However, its construction was incredibly advanced, while the power and performance on offer marked it out from just about every other contemporary production car. Unfortunately so did the price, which is why just 1400 Gullwings were built – along with another 1858 Roadsters. Despite its legendary status, the Gullwing could be very tricky to drive, which is why the open car that superseded it featured fresh suspension that ensured the handling was much more predictable near the limit.

Statistics

Price	£4329
0–62mph	8.8sec
0–100mph	15sec (est)
Max speed	140mph (224kph)
Engine type	In-line six
Engine capacity	2996cc
Bore x stroke	85mm x 88mm
Max power	241bhp @ 6100rpm
Max torque	217lb ft @ 4800rpm
Power to weight ratio	186bhp per tonne
Transmission	Four-speed manual, rear-wheel drive
Kerb weight	1293kg
Length	4463mm
Width	1793mm
Height	1300mm
Fuel consumption	18.4mpg
Year introduced	1954

Mercedes
CL65 AMG
Brutal coupé from Stuttgart

Mercedes
CL65 AMG

Brutal coupé from Stuttgart

This isn't the first CL65 AMG to come from the Mercedes stable, and arguably the first edition (from 2003) is more of a looker. What you can't argue with is what the post-2007 CL65 offers – which is phenomenal performance married to astonishing refinement. Indeed, the car is so powerful and offers so much torque, that Merc's seven-speed automatic gearbox can't cope, meaning this edition of the CL has to make do with the stronger five-speed transmission. All of which begs the question of why Mercedes ever built this car in the first place; the entry-level CL500 is so capable that any extra horsepower or gadgetry is frankly unnecessary. That doesn't stop the CL65 from being a technological tour de force though.

Statistics

Price	£149,565
0–62mph	4.4sec
0–100mph	8sec (est)
Max speed	155mph (248kph)
Engine type	V12
Engine capacity	5980cc
Bore x stroke	82.6mm x 93mm
Max power	604bhp @ 4800rpm
Max torque	737lb ft @ 2000rpm
Power to weight ratio	270bhp per tonne
Transmission	Five-speed auto, rear-wheel drive
Kerb weight	2240kg
Length	5065mm
Width	1871mm
Height	1419mm
Fuel consumption	19.1mpg
Year introduced	2007

Mercedes
CLK GT-R

The million-pound road car

Mercedes
CLK GT-R

The million-pound road car

You'd be entitled to expect something pretty special if you were spending £1.1m on a new car, and that's just what CLK GT-R owners got. With production limited to just 25 units, the GT-R was created with one aim in mind: to win Le Mans. Unfortunately the car never achieved this, as the aerodynamics led to the car getting airborne at high speeds. Despite this, the Merc was incredibly well engineered, because it was as safe and clean as any regular production CLK. And although the GT-R didn't win Le Mans, it did phenomenally well in the DTM race series, winning all 11 races of 1998.

Statistics

Price	£1.1m
0–62mph	3.8sec
0–100mph	7sec (est)
Max speed	199mph (318kph)
Engine type	V12
Engine capacity	6898cc
Bore x stroke	89.0mm x 92.4mm
Max power	612bhp @ 6800rpm
Max torque	572lb ft @ 5250rpm
Power to weight ratio	416bhp per tonne
Transmission	Six-speed manual, rear-wheel drive
Kerb weight	1470kg
Length	4855mm
Width	1950mm
Height	1164mm
Fuel consumption	13.1mpg
Year introduced	1998

MG
Metro 6R4

The world's fastest shopping trolley

MG
Metro 6R4

The world's fastest shopping trolley

E651 BJN

Like the Audi Quattro Sport and Ford RS200, the 6R4 was a Group B special that was obsolete before it was even fully developed. And like all those other Group B monsters, the Metro was ludicrously fast thanks to its mid-mounted 3-litre V6 and four-wheel drive. Indeed, when *Autocar* magazine tested a race-spec 6R4, the car proved to the quickest machine it had ever driven, capable of sprinting to 60mph in little more than three seconds – a record which it held for years afterwards. The available performance helped little though; the cars proved virtually unsaleable on the open market, and Austin-Rover walked away as soon as the Group B series was cancelled.

Statistics

Price	£34,783
0–62mph	4.5sec
0–100mph	12.8sec
Max speed	140mph (224kph)
Engine type	V6
Engine capacity	2991cc
Bore x stroke	92mm x 75mm
Max power	250bhp @ 7000rpm
Max torque	225lb ft @ 6500rpm
Power to weight ratio	243bhp per tonne
Transmission	Five-speed manual, four-wheel drive
Kerb weight	1030kg
Length	3350mm
Width	1880mm
Height	1500mm
Fuel consumption	18mpg
Year introduced	1985

Mosler
MT900S

A true race car for the road

Mosler
MT900S

A true race car for the road

Take every supercar design cliché going, blend them together, and you end up with the Mosler MT900. If that sounds critical it's not meant to; this is one mean-looking machine that has the go to match the show, thanks to a Corvette Z06 V8 in the middle, driving the rear wheels via a Porsche 911 GT2 gearbox. Developed on the race track, the Mosler's carbon-fibre bodyshell is packed with cutting-edge technology such as titanium springs in the suspension, thin-wall subframes and magnesium wheels. That's why it's so fast, but the figures here are for the standard car; opt for the more extreme MT900SC and you'll get 0–100mph in just 6.5 seconds. Fast enough for you?

Statistics

Price	£130,000
0–62mph	3.7sec
0–100mph	7.5sec
Max speed	190mph (304kph)
Engine type	V8
Engine capacity	5665cc
Bore x stroke	99mm x 92mm
Max power	406bhp @ 6000rpm
Max torque	400lb ft @ 4800rpm
Power to weight ratio	451bhp per tonne
Transmission	Six-speed manual, rear-wheel drive
Kerb weight	900kg
Length	4800mm
Width	2006mm
Height	1074mm
Fuel consumption	15mpg
Year introduced	2004

Nissan
GT-R

Performance has never been more usable

Nissan
GT-R

Performance has never been more usable

Nissan's Skyline GT-Rs were always deeply impressive cars, but this new GT-R is truly something else; the name is the only thing shared with anything the Japanese company has ever built before. For starters there's now a twin-turbo V6 up front, while the paddle shift-controlled transaxle also incorporates technology that allows the driver to select how aggressive the changes are as well as when they take place. With massive power, four-wheel drive and a price tag considerably lower than rivals such as the BMW M3 and Porsche 911, it's hard to see how Nissan's factory will be able to keep up with demand.

Statistics

Price	£55,000
0–62mph	3.5sec
0–100mph	7.5sec (est)
Max speed	194mph (310kph)
Engine type	V6
Engine capacity	3799cc
Bore x stroke	95.5mm x 88.4mm
Max power	473bhp @ 6400rpm
Max torque	434lb ft @ 3200rpm
Power to weight ratio	249bhp per tonne
Transmission	Six-speed semi-auto, four-wheel drive
Kerb weight	1740kg
Length	4655mm
Width	1895mm
Height	1370mm
Fuel consumption	21mpg (est)
Year introduced	2008

Nissan
R390

Thought the GT-R was fast?

R390 NIS

Nissan
R390

Thought the GT-R was fast?

Another project that got the green light solely with the aim of winning Le Mans, the R390's motorsport career proved something of a disaster, as the cars weren't reliable enough to last the race. In sales terms the R390 also proved less than successful, as just one road-going example was built, to comply with GT racing rules – and Nissan clearly lost a packet on the project. But with those looks and engineering, the car is a definite winner in the supercar stakes and there can be no doubt that it deserves to be included here because no Nissan has ever been more extreme.

Price	£1m
0–62mph	3.9sec
0–100mph	9.0sec
Max speed	175mph (280kph)
Engine type	V8
Engine capacity	3500cc
Bore x stroke	85mm x 77mm
Max power	539bhp @ 6800rpm
Max torque	470lb ft @ 4400rpm
Power to weight ratio	435bhp per tonne
Transmission	Six-speed sequential manual, rear-wheel drive
Kerb weight	1240kg
Length	4720mm
Width	2000mm
Height	1140mm
Fuel consumption	15mpg
Year introduced	1998

Pagani
Zonda Roadster

Mean and roofless

Pagani
Zonda Roadster

Mean and roofless

Horacio Pagani came from nowhere in 1999, to launch his own supercar company – and where others have failed this Italian concern has thrived. It helped that Pagani already had links with Ferrari and Lamborghini, for whom he'd undertaken specialist composite work for their lightweight bodyshells; such experience was essential for the Zonda, named after a wind from the Andes. At first there was a 7-litre Mercedes-sourced V12, but from 2002 there was also a 7.3-litre edition offered to make the Zonda even faster. However, it was when the Roadster was unveiled in 2003 that the car became seriously exhilarating to drive, thanks to its 200mph+ top speed.

Statistics

Price	£380,000
0–62mph	3.7sec
0–100mph	7.4sec (est)
Max speed	200mph (320kph)
Engine type	V12
Engine capacity	7291cc
Bore x stroke	91.5mm x 92.4mm
Max power	555bhp @ 5900rpm
Max torque	553lb ft @ 4050rpm
Power to weight ratio	434bhp per tonne
Transmission	Six-speed manual, rear-wheel drive
Kerb weight	1280kg
Length	4395mm
Width	2055mm
Height	1151mm
Fuel consumption	13mpg (est)
Year introduced	2003

Peugeot
205 T16

French fancy for the rough

Peugeot
205 T16

French fancy for the rough

Probably the best-looking of all the Group B specials, the 205 T16 looked much like Peugeot's regular shopping trolley, but it was both longer and wider. Not only that, but no regular production 205 ever packed a 200bhp powerplant behind the driver, which in race form could be tuned to give 500bhp. The construction was also quite unlike any other 205's, with plenty of composites to keep the weight down, while there was a trick four-wheel drive system. It was just a shame that the transverse location of the four-cylinder engine led to some decidely tricky handling characteristics when the car was on the limit...

Statistics

Price	£25,000
0–62mph	7.8sec
0–100mph	21.7sec
Max speed	128mph (205kph)
Engine type	In-line four
Engine capacity	1775cc
Bore x stroke	83mm x 82mm
Max power	200bhp @ 5750rpm
Max torque	188lb ft @ 4000rpm
Power to weight ratio	181bhp per tonne
Transmission	Five-speed manual, four-wheel drive
Kerb weight	1105kg
Length	3820mm
Width	1700mm
Height	1353mm
Fuel consumption	29.8mpg
Year introduced	1984

Porsche
911 GT2 (997)

Building the perfect beast

Porsche
911 GT2 (997)

Building the perfect beast

S·GO 1320

Improving on the 997 Turbo was never going to be an easy task for the boffins at Porsche, but somehow they've managed to do it. Although the Turbo is an amazing machine, the third edition of the GT2 trounces it thanks to an extra 50bhp, achieved through letting the engine breathe much better. It's also lost weight thanks to the elimination of four-wheel drive; the GT2's 523 horses are all corralled to the rear axle. To help keep the thing on the road there's a limited-slip differential along with traction control and electronic damper management – but the car can still be a bit of a handful in inexperienced hands!

Statistics

Price	£131,070
0–62mph	3.7sec
0–100mph	7.4sec
Max speed	204mph (326kph)
Engine type	Flat-six
Engine capacity	3600cc
Bore x stroke	100mm x 76.4mm
Max power	523bhp @ 6500rpm
Max torque	502lb ft @ 2200rpm
Power to weight ratio	363bhp per tonne
Transmission	Six-speed manual, rear-wheel drive
Kerb weight	1440kg
Length	4747mm
Width	1991mm
Height	1413mm
Fuel consumption	22.6mpg
Year introduced	2008

S·GO 1320

Renault
A610

Plastic fantastic

Renault
A610

Plastic fantastic

Alpine A610

If this car had worn Porsche badges, the factory wouldn't have been able to keep up with demand. But because it was a Renault, the A610 never stood a chance. Driving the rear wheels was a potent V6, located behind the cabin, while the bodywork was all plastic to keep weight and costs down. The stiff chassis was fabulously set up, giving superb handling, while the bodywork was beautiful without being brash. Fast, affordable, practical and reliable, the A610 offered so many things that other supercars couldn't – yet buyers chose to spend their money on rivals such as the Porsche 944 instead. Tragic.

Statistics

Price	£39,550
0–62mph	5.8sec
0–100mph	16.0sec
Max speed	159mph (254kph)
Engine type	V6
Engine capacity	2975cc
Bore x stroke	93mm x 73mm
Max power	250bhp @ 5750rpm
Max torque	258lb ft @ 2900rpm
Power to weight ratio	181bhp per tonne
Transmission	Five-speed manual, rear-wheel drive
Kerb weight	1380kg
Length	4415mm
Width	1762mm
Height	1188mm
Fuel consumption	24.4mpg
Year introduced	1992

Saleen
S7

Pokey, powerful and pricey

Saleen
S7

Pokey, powerful and pricey

Engineered in the UK, but built in the US, the Saleen is named after its founder Steve Saleen, who made his name tuning Mustangs for racing; it was just a matter of time before he made his own fully fledged supercar. That time came in 2002, when the S7 made its debut, with just 500bhp. In 2005 a twin-turbo edition was released, to stay one step ahead of the supercar pack. Whereas most hypercars feature cutting-edge technology, the S7 is relatively low-tech in that there's a glassfibre and carbon-fibre bodyshell over a tubular steel spaceframe, which houses a pushrod V8. Simple it might be, but it's also damned effective and ferociously quick!

Statistics

Price	$580,000
0–62mph	2.8sec
0–100mph	5.9sec
Max speed	240mph (384kph) (claimed)
Engine type	V8
Engine capacity	6998cc
Bore x stroke	104.8mm x 101.6mm
Max power	750bhp @ 6300rpm
Max torque	700lb ft @ 4800rpm
Power to weight ratio	560bhp per tonne
Transmission	Six-speed manual, rear-wheel drive
Kerb weight	1338kg
Length	4774mm
Width	1990mm
Height	1041mm
Fuel consumption	12mpg (est)
Year introduced	2005

Spyker
C8 Aileron

Going Dutch

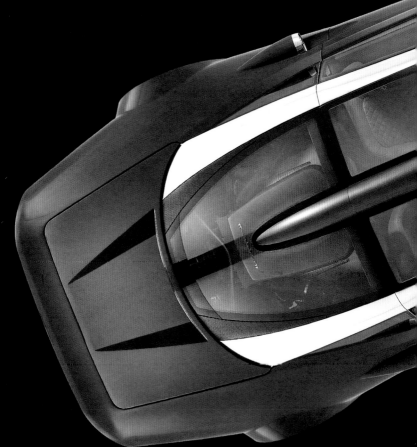

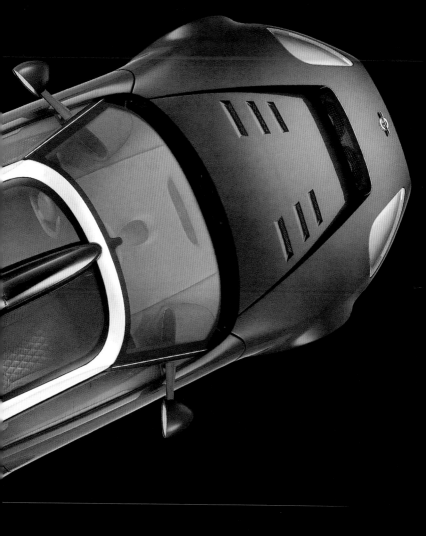

Spyker
C8 Aileron

Going Dutch

If you like your supercars on the ornate side, the Spyker will
be right up your street. Ever since the Dutch outfit burst onto
the scene in 2000 with its Spyder, it has gained a reputation for
creating some of the most lavish car interiors ever seen. The
Aileron uses Spyker's earlier Laviolette as a start point, but adds
10cm to the wheelbase, to increase torsional rigidity by 40 per cent,
improving the handling in the process – it looks like the old car, but
Spyker claims this is effectively a second-generation C8. There's
also now the option of an automatic gearbox, with motive power
still provided by a 400bhp Audi V8 behind the cabin.

Statistics

Price	€200,000
0–62mph	4.5sec
0–100mph	8.5sec (est)
Max speed	187mph (300kph)
Engine type	V8
Engine capacity	4172cc
Bore x stroke	84.5mm x 93mm
Max power	400bhp @ 7000rpm
Max torque	354lb ft @ 3400rpm
Power to weight ratio	281bhp per tonne
Transmission	Six-speed manual/auto, rear-wheel drive
Kerb weight	1425kg
Length	4561mm
Width	1910mm
Height	1214mm
Fuel consumption	24mpg
Year introduced	2008

SPYKER

Spyker
D12 Peking to Paris

Formula 1 goes off-roading

D12 Peking to Paris

Spyker
D12 Peking to Paris

Formula 1 goes off-roading

If you want to show two fingers to the environmentalists, there's
no better way of doing it than by driving a Spyker D12. Combining
the company's typical over-the-top design flair with an amazing
pillarless SUV bodyshell, the D12 has an aluminium space frame to
keep weight down while also maximising torsional rigidity. Spyker
has also thrown all the technology it can at the D12, with ceramic
brake discs along with a VW-sourced W12 engine, F1-style
gearbox and permanent four-wheel drive. In the process it has
created possibly the world fastest and most luxurious off-roader
– although it's hard to imagine many owners taking their cars into
the rough stuff.

Statistics

Price	£190,000
0–62mph	5.0sec
0–100mph	9.5sec (est)
Max speed	187mph (300kph)
Engine type	W12
Engine capacity	5998cc
Bore x stroke	84mm x 90.2mm
Max power	500bhp
Max torque	450lb ft
Power to weight ratio	270bhp per tonne
Transmission	Six-speed semi-auto, four-wheel drive
Kerb weight	1850kg
Length	4950mm
Width	2000mm
Height	1680–1775mm
Fuel consumption	20mpg
Year introduced	2006

Shelby Supercars
Ultimate Aero TT

It's officially faster than a Veyron...

Shelby Supercars
Ultimate Aero TT

It's officially faster than a Veyron...

While Bugatti's Veyron grabs all the headlines about being the world's fastest car, America's SSC Ultimate Aero has been officially timed at 256mph with the promise of a potential 273mph, thanks to a twin-turbo V8 that started out as a 5.7-litre Corvette unit. Despite this, the Ultimate Aero costs less than half as much as a Veyron, so is Bugatti simply profiteering? Probably not; the SSC may pack the world's most powerful engine (at least in a standard road car), but it doesn't have the sheer class or build quality of the Veyron – but then you'll be going too fast to notice those anyway...

Statistics

Price	£335,000
0–60mph	2.8sec
0–100mph	7.0sec (est)
Max speed	256mph (410kph)
Engine type	V8
Engine capacity	6342cc
Bore x stroke	104.8mm x 91.9mm
Max power	1183bhp @ 6950rpm
Max torque	1094lb ft @ 6150rpm
Power to weight ratio	946bhp per tonne
Transmission	Six-speed manual, rear-wheel drive
Kerb weight	1250kg
Length	4475mm
Width	2101mm
Height	1092mm
Fuel consumption	12mpg (est)
Year introduced	2007

TVR
Cerbera

TVR moves into the big time

TVR
Cerbera

TVR moves into the big time

TVR had long offered masses of performance for surprisingly little money, but the Cerbera moved the game on for this tiny British car maker. Not only did the Cerbera pack TVR's first in-house engine, but it also took the company into the major supercar league, in terms of cost as well as performance. Offered as a two-door coupé only, the Cerbera was spectacularly fast in V8 form; even the straight-six that later became available gave quicker acceleration than anything offered by Ferrari or Porsche. TVR even looked at building an 880bhp V12 edition – but saw sense before giving the project the green light.

Statistics

Price	£45,000
0–62mph	4.3sec
0–100mph	9.2sec
Max speed	180mph (288kph)
Engine type	V8
Engine capacity	4185cc
Bore x stroke	91mm x 86mm
Max power	350bhp @ 6500rpm
Max torque	320lb ft @ 4500rpm
Power to weight ratio	323bhp per tonne
Transmission	Five-speed manual, rear-wheel drive
Kerb weight	1178kg
Length	4280mm
Width	1865mm
Height	1220mm
Fuel consumption	19.8mpg
Year introduced	1996

Vauxhall
VX220 Turbo

Who needs an Elise?

AP02 XOB

Vauxhall
VX220 Turbo

Who needs an Elise?

If you're going to base your brand-building sportster on anything, a Lotus Elise is a pretty good place to start. That's exactly what Vauxhall reckoned anyway, when the fabulous image-building VX220 arrived in 2000. Surprisingly different from the Elise that sired it, the VX220 was raw and focused, and decently quick – but the Turbo that arrived in 2003 was a monster of a machine, capable of taking on far more costly supercars and eating them for breakfast. With pace, poise and a low price, the VX220 Turbo had everything the enthusiast driver could want – except a posh badge on the nose, which is why the car never sold as well as it should have done.

Statistics

Price	£25,495
0–62mph	4.9sec
0–100mph	12.6sec
Max speed	151mph (242kph)
Engine type	In-line four
Engine capacity	1998cc
Bore x stroke	86mm x 86mm
Max power	197bhp @ 5500rpm
Max torque	184lb ft @ 1950rpm
Power to weight ratio	212bhp per tonne
Transmission	Five-speed manual, rear-wheel drive
Kerb weight	930kg
Length	3786mm
Width	1880mm
Height	1117mm
Fuel consumption	33mpg
Year introduced	2003

Vector
W8

The supercar built to aircraft standards

Vector W8

The supercar built to aircraft standards

There's a school of thought that says America's only proper supercar is the Corvette. However, not only are there others in these very pages, but in the 1990s there was another contender: the Vector W8. As long ago as 1977 the Vector Aeromotive W2 debuted, its designer Gerry Wiegert being obsessed with aeronautical technology – which is why the car was priced at $420,000 when it finally went on sale as the W8 in 1991. At the heart of the W8 was a turbocharged 600bhp 6-litre V8, supposedly giving a 200mph top speed. Despite the price tag, 14 were sold before the car was superseded by the WX-3 in 1992 – priced at $765,000!

Statistics

Price	£216,703
0–62mph	4.2sec
0–100mph	8.3sec
Max speed	218mph (349kph)
Engine type	V8
Engine capacity	5973cc
Bore x stroke	101.6mm x 92.1mm
Max power	625bhp @ 5700rpm
Max torque	630lb ft @ 4900rpm
Power to weight ratio	414bhp per tonne
Transmission	Three-speed auto, rear-wheel drive
Kerb weight	1669kg
Length	4369mm
Width	1930mm
Height	1080mm
Fuel consumption	15mpg
Year introduced	1991

Volkswagen
W12

The most powerful VW ever

Volkswagen
W12
The most powerful VW ever

When the W12 made its debut, Volkswagen claimed it was a one-off, but the car could be made available in limited numbers. Most commentators thought the car was fantastic – but the Volkswagen badges didn't help. Perhaps that was enough to scupper the project, but it didn't die very quickly because at the 1998 Geneva motor show a roadster version was unveiled and at the 2002 Geneva motor show both ItalDesign and Volkswagen had a W12 coupé on their stands. But soon after it was revealed, the project was dead – VW/Audi had enough supercars with the Bugatti Veyron as well as two new Lamborghinis (the Murciélago and Gallardo).

Statistics

Price	N/A
0–62mph	3.5sec
0–100mph	7sec (est)
Max speed	217mph (350kph)
Engine type	W12
Engine capacity	5998cc
Bore x stroke	84mm x 90.2mm
Max power	590bhp @ 7000rpm
Max torque	457lb ft @ 5800rpm
Power to weight ratio	492bhp per tonne
Transmission	Six-speed sequential manual, four-wheel drive
Kerb weight	1200kg
Length	4500mm
Width	1920mm
Height	1100mm
Fuel consumption	16mpg (est)
Year introduced	2001

Yamaha
OX99-11
It could have toppled McLaren's F1

Yamaha
OX99-11

It could have toppled McLaren's F1

In the world of the supercar, the term 'race car for the road' is usually marketing hype, but in the case of the Yamaha it was truly deserved. That's why it's tragic that it never made production; it's one of the few cars that could have given the Mclaren F1 some grief. The OX99-11 appeared in 1992, with a 420bhp 3.5-litre V12 in the middle of the car, a detuned version of the powerplant fitted to the Brabhams and Jordans of the early 1990s. The price was an eye-watering $1m, but where else could you get anything like it? Just three were built before the project was abandoned.

Statistics

Price	$1m
0–62mph	3.1sec
0–100mph	7sec (est)
Max speed	219mph (304kph)
Engine type	V12
Engine capacity	3498cc
Bore x stroke	N/A
Max power	420bhp @ 10,000rpm
Max torque	N/A
Power to weight ratio	420bhp per tonne
Transmission	Six-speed manual, rear-wheel drive
Kerb weight	1000kg
Length	4400mm
Width	2000mm
Height	1220mm
Fuel consumption	14mpg (est)
Year introduced	1992

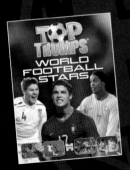

Great new
Top Trumps packs!

CLASSICS Dinosaurs • Ultimate Military Jets • Skyscrapers • The Dog
• World Football Stars • Wonders of the World • British Army Fighting Forces
• Wildlife in Danger • Gumball 3000 Custom Cars

SPECIALS Roald Dahl • Star Wars 1-3 • Star Wars 4-6 • Star Wars
Starships • Star Wars Clone Wars • Horror • High School Musical • MotoGP
• Pirates of the Caribbean • Dr Who 2 • Dr Who 3 • The Simpsons Classic
Volume 1 • The Simpsons Classic Volume 2 • Bratz Passion for Fashion
• WWE2 • Jacqueline Wilson • Transformers • Marvel Max • Harry Potter and
the Order of the Phoenix • Top Gear • DC Super Heroes • DC Super Heroes 2

SPORTS Newcastle FC • Tottenham Hotspur FC • Chelsea FC
• Man United FC • Arsenal FC • Liverpool FC • Football Legends

Play Top Trumps at
TOPTRUMPS.COM